IT'S THE END OF THE WORLD!

CLIMATE CHANGE

BY LISA OWINGS

BELLWETHER MEDIA • MINNEAPOLIS, MN

Are you ready to take it to the extreme? Torque books thrust you into the action-packed world of sports, vehicles, mystery, and adventure. These books may include dirt, smoke, fire, and chilling tales. **WARNING**: read at your own risk.

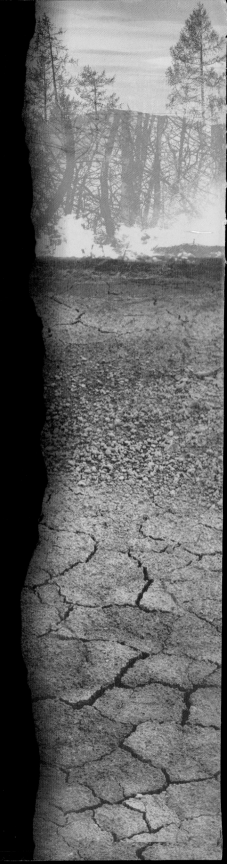

This edition first published in 2020 by Bellwether Media, Inc.

No part of this publication may be reproduced in whole or in part without written permission of the publisher.
For information regarding permission, write to Bellwether Media, Inc.,
Attention: Permissions Department,
6012 Blue Circle Drive, Minnetonka, MN 55343.

Library of Congress Cataloging-in-Publication Data

Names: Owings, Lisa, author.
Title: Climate Change / by Lisa Owings.
Description: Minneapolis, MN : Bellwether Media, Inc., [2020] | Series:
    Torque: It's the End of the World! | Audience: Ages 7-12. | Audience:
    Grades 3 to 7. | Includes bibliographical references and index.
Identifiers: LCCN 2019000936 (print) | LCCN 2019007408 (ebook) |
    ISBN 9781618917201 (ebook) | ISBN 9781644870808
    (hardcover : alk. paper)
Subjects: LCSH: Climatic changes–Juvenile literature. | Global warming–
    Juvenile literature. | Nature–Effect of human beings on–Juvenile literature.
Classification: LCC QC903.15 (ebook) | LCC QC903.15 .0945 2020 (print) |
    DDC 363.738/74–dc23
LC record available at https://lccn.loc.gov/2019000936

Editor: Rebecca Sabelko   Designer: Andrea Schneider

Printed in the United States of America, North Mankato, MN.

TABLE OF CONTENTS

HEAT WAVE

This heat is getting old! You have been stuck inside for weeks. But the power is turned off each afternoon to reduce **emissions**.

Sweat drenches your clothes. You press a towel to your forehead for relief. Your baby sister is crying again. She is not handling the heat well. Your parents are worried.

THE DEADLIEST WEATHER

More than 600 Americans die from heat every year. That is more than most other natural disasters combined!

You ask your dad if you can have more water. Each family is allowed a certain amount each day. He says he is not thirsty and hands you his glass.

You check the weather as the power returns. There is no change in sight. The news says you may need to **evacuate** if the heat lasts. It may not be possible to live here in a few years.

GOING WITHOUT

In the future, some areas may need to limit energy or water use.

A CHANGING WORLD

Climate change is a pattern of rising temperatures around the world. It has happened naturally throughout Earth's history. But around the early 1900s, temperatures began warming faster than ever before. Studies show humans are to blame!

WHAT HAPPENS WHEN THE ARCTIC THAWS?

Methane is a greenhouse gas found in the frozen ground of the Arctic. Methane is released into the atmosphere when the Arctic ground thaws. The increased amount of methane could cause temperatures to rise even higher!

FLOODING

Climate change pushes temperatures to rise and melt the Earth's **ice caps**. Seas flood coastal cities. **Natural disasters** hit harder and more often. People are unable to live in some areas.

Some animals face **extinction** as Earth changes. Even humans have a hard time learning to **adapt**. It gets harder to grow food and find water. Some **diseases** spread more easily.

DYING REEFS: CORAL BLEACHING

Corals get their color from plantlike algae. Algae leaves when oceans warm. Coral turns white and often dies.

CHAIN REACTION

ice caps melt

sea levels rise

natural disasters
destroy cities

temperatures rise to
levels unfit for human life

Scientists are studying ways to keep climate change under control. Can we turn back the clock? Or will we be forced to survive in a **hostile** world?

SHIFTING THE BALANCE

People have used machines that run on **fossil fuels** since the mid-1700s. These fuels release **greenhouse gases** when they are burned.

GREENHOUSE GAS EMISSIONS

Greenhouse gases take in some of the Sun's heat. They trap the heat in Earth's **atmosphere**. These gases are not harmful at natural levels. But humans have increased greenhouse gases to dangerously high levels.

SAVING OUR FORESTS

Forests store a lot of carbon dioxide. This greenhouse gas is released when forests are destroyed. Saving Earth's forests can help fight climate change.

In the 1970s, scientists began studying how humans affect climate. **Data** has shown a large jump in Earth's temperature. Scientists now agree humans caused it.

SCIENTISTS COLLECTING DATA

Earth's temperature has increased about 1.6 degrees Fahrenheit (0.9 degrees Celsius) since 1901. Temperatures could increase several more degrees by the end of the century.

Earth is warming too quickly. Life has not had time to get ready for these changes. Scientists now warn that we are at a turning point.

MOST CARS USE FOSSIL FUELS

55 MILLION YEARS AGO

Earth's temperature rose about 9 degrees Fahrenheit (5 degrees Celsius). Scientists think a large amount of methane gas was released from the sea. Many types of life went extinct. The PETM helps scientists understand current climate change.

Humans still use fossil fuels every day. This causes greenhouse gas levels to increase each year. We need to do more to stop climate change. We may not be able to repair the damage if we fail.

BEFORE IT IS TOO LATE

Many countries have worked together to reduce greenhouse gas emissions since the 1990s. The Kyoto Protocol **treaty** was created in 1997. Several countries agreed to reduce emissions.

World leaders reached the Paris Agreement in 2016. They promised to keep warming under 3.6 degrees Fahrenheit (2 degrees Celsius).

WORLD LEADERS CELEBRATING
AFTER THE PARIS AGREEMENT

IN THE MEDIA

DOCUMENTARY TITLE:

AN INCONVENIENT TRUTH

YEAR RELEASED: 2006

Former Vice President Al Gore tried to inform people about the dangers of climate change. He spread the truth about global warming. He wanted to create change before it was too late!

Global emissions are still rising. We are unlikely to undo all the damage. But we have a chance to stop things from getting worse.

You can fight for change in your own home and community. Ride your bike. Plant trees. Create less waste. We have a chance to save life on Earth!

GLOSSARY

adapt—to change over a long period of time

atmosphere—the gases that surround Earth

climate—the average weather of a place over a long period of time

data—facts or information

diseases—illnesses

emissions—gases, chemicals, or other substances released into the atmosphere

evacuate—to move away from a dangerous area

extinction—the state of not existing

fossil fuels—fuels such as coal, oil, and natural gas that were formed in the Earth from plant or animal remains

greenhouse gases—gases such as carbon dioxide and methane that trap heat in Earth's atmosphere

hostile—unfriendly or unwelcoming

ice caps—the large, thick sheets of ice that cover the North and South Poles

natural disasters—sudden events in nature that cause great harm

treaty—a formal written agreement between countries

TO LEARN MORE

AT THE LIBRARY

Dickmann, Nancy. *Using Renewable Energy*. New York, N.Y.: Crabtree Publishing Company, 2018.

Dykstra, Mary A. *Climate Change and Extreme Storms*. Minneapolis, Minn.: Lerner Publications, 2019.

Herman, Gail. *What Is Climate Change?* New York, N.Y.: Penguin Workshop, 2018.

ON THE WEB

FACTSURFER

Factsurfer.com gives you a safe, fun way to find more information.
1. Go to www.factsurfer.com
2. Enter "climate change" into the search box and click Q.
3. Select your book cover to see a list of related web sites.

INDEX

The images in this book are reproduced through the courtesy of: Beautiful landscape, front cover (before town); Albina Tiplyashina, front cover, pp. 2-3 (after town); Nopparat Promtha, front cover, pp. 2-3 (after town flames); Evgeny Haritonov, front cover, pp. 2-3 (after town skull); Nusara Promsiri, pp. 4-5 (girl); Plindyk Iuliia, pp. 4-5 (city); TWStock, pp. 6-7; Silken Photography, pp. 8-9; aquapix, pp. 10-11; Crystal Knihniski, p. 11 (top left); Tanguy de Saint-Cry, p. 11 (bottom left); shiji ao, p. 11 (top right); Mykola Mazuryk, p. 11 (bottom right); Steve Allen, p. 12 (greenhouse gas inset); nasidastudio, pp. 12-13; National Geographic Image Collection/ Alamy, pp. 14-15; Piyaset, p. 15 (inset); TierneyMJ, pp. 16-17; Bernhard Staehli, p. 17 (PETM inset); COP21/ Alamy, pp. 18-19; Sergey Novikov, pp. 20-21; AF archive/ Alamy, p. 20 (Al Gore); Ink Drop, p. 21 (protest inset).